The Twinless Twin

A tale of bereavement and enlightenment for those who have lost their twin...

J.H. Lutz

ISBN 978-1-64670-657-0 (Paperback)
ISBN 978-1-64670-658-7 (Hardcover)
ISBN 978-1-64670-659-4 (Digital)

Covenant Books, Inc.
11661 Hwy 707
Murrells Inlet, SC 29576
www.covenantbooks.com

DEDICATION

This book is dedicated, first, to my twin sister, Georgia, and all those whose soul contracts made them a part of such an Historical event. My heart grieves for each one who participated, for this was a lifetime impact. But this tragic event spurred a commitment to learn exactly why we have been created. I thank you for these lessons, and I love you all.

I first gave my account to Dr. Raymond Brandt, the editor of TWINLESS TWINS MAGAZINE back around 1999. Of course, at the time I only had the first part of the story—the actual accident that happened. I told Dr. Brandt that after the event, I went into a fog for 4 years, but when I emerged, fully awake again, I knew right away that Georgia was all right-she wasn't dead, all was well with the world, and two angels were on either side of me holding me up. Dr. Brandt got so excited that he called me early in the morning two days after he had received my email. He said that I must write about what happened during the four years that I was "away." The story was not complete until I found out why I had emerged from the fog with so positive an attitude. His encouragement prompted me to reach deep within, and the rest of the tale took form.

And this book might not have been printed if my wonderful husband, Chuck, and daughter, Tarrin, had not pushed me to get it published. Tarrin also helped me create the audio CD, recording it herself.

Putting pen to paper has released the healing process that never took place when I was a child. I hope my book inspires and brings comfort to all those who have lost one so dear to them.

Jennifer H. Lutz

GEORGIA RUTH

My Twin looks down from far away,
It is early dawn;
And as the sun unfolds its arms,
I think, "She's been gone so very long."

But then I hear her call to me
As color floods the sky;
"I'm sorry for what I put you through,
But it was decided before you and I.

You knew I couldn't stay too long—
I had other work to do!
But still you insisted, and I went along;
I loved you so very much, too!

So I am busy way up here,
And you are busy, too.
We have our work cut out for us
Before the day is through.

But we will be together again,
When the sun unfolds its arms.
On another day, another dawn;
It won't be very long.

For time goes by so very fast!
We both have chores to do.
We must complete them on our time,
Before your life is through.

You will always be my sister,
And I'll be there for you.
I love you, my twin—I always will,
And I'll meet you when you're through."

The sun enfolds me in its warmth,
Another day is here;
And I will complete my chores today,
And all throughout my years.

Then we will meet at Heaven's Gate,
As the dawn unfolds so bright!
And my twin and I will be together again—
In God's eternal Light.

Jennie Lee felt a sadness in her heart. The whole school was celebrating because there were five sets of identical twins in the Newburn Elementary School at the same time! A man from the *Newburn Daily News* had come to the school to interview each set of twins and take their pictures for the paper. Why, there were even identical twin sisters who had older twin sisters! In Jennie Lee's eighth grade classroom, there were two sets of twin boys! Mr. Roy, the principal, had the twins line up and march across the stage for everyone to see.

After the ceremony, all the classes went to lunch. The whole cafeteria was buzzing about the twins. Everyone was very happy that their school had so many sets of identical twins at the same time. The boys and girls in each class were especially proud of their twin classmates.

As Jennie Lee picked up her lunch, she turned to Julie Baker in line behind her. "I was an identical twin once," she whispered.

"Oh, you're lying," Julie said. "You just can't stand to see them getting attention."

Julie turned away in a huff to go and sit with her friends. "It is *too* true!" Jennie Lee's mind screamed as she fought back the tears that were about to spill down her cheeks. Her heart was pounding. "We could have been the sixth pair of twins! Georgia, I miss you," she sniffed back the tears and sat down.

Yes, it was true. Jennie Lee had been born an identical twin, and this is her story. Jennie Lee didn't talk about her twin because Georgia had been tucked away in her heart for nine years. None of the children knew because her sister had died before they started school. Jennie Lee felt true loneliness since Georgia Ruth had passed away. She couldn't remember what it was like to be together, but she did know that her life was very different now, and that half of her seemed missing.

You see, Jennie Lee and Georgia Ruth had been born identical twins. That means they grew in the very same sack inside their mother's womb. They were born on the very same day, just minutes apart—two peas in a pod!

They had the same hair color; they had the same eye color; why, they looked exactly like each other!

Everyone in the family was very proud of the twins. They were the first twins born in the Anna Maria Hospital in a very long time. And they were the first twins born in the Hilton family in many, many years. Everybody in town celebrated with Mr. and Mrs. Hilton when the twins were born. When Mrs. Hilton pushed the twins in their carriage, people would always stop and say, "Oh look, here comes the twins!" Everybody in Newburn was very happy for Mr. and Mrs. Hilton.

Jennie Lee and Georgia Ruth had their own way of communicating that other people couldn't understand. The twins had their own special language. Sometimes they didn't even need to talk out loud, they just knew what each other was thinking. They looked alike, dressed alike, and played alike! The twins were always together, and they were very happy to have each other.

One day, just before the girls' fifth birthday, all this changed. Georgia Ruth died. She didn't mean to die, but sometimes accidents happen. Sometimes people die when they are young instead of old. Sometimes a twin dies.

It was a beautiful spring day. The twins played outside all that morning. They were visiting with their favorite uncle, then said goodbye when it happened. Georgia Ruth got down on her knees behind a truck. Jennie Lee didn't know why her twin did this. Jennie Lee thought something had rolled under the truck; perhaps Georgia Ruth reached out to pick it up. In the flash of an instant, the truck had rolled back. Georgia Ruth was hit! Then, she was gone from this world.

The whole town felt very sad. "How could this happen?" they asked. Nobody knew how to comfort Mr. and Mrs. Hilton. Nobody knew what to do for the family. Everybody asked how God could let this happen. Jennie Lee didn't know what happened either. One minute, she had been standing beside her twin, the next minute, her twin crawled behind the truck. Jennie Lee couldn't remember her sister doing this. She never saw Georgia Ruth going toward the truck. The twins had never been separated before, and Jennie Lee couldn't understand why this happened.

In an instant, the twins' lives changed forever. One minute, Jennie Lee had a twin sister, and the next minute, she was running up the driveway, calling to her grandmother, "Grammy! Grammy! Georgia's been hit! I think she's dead!" What made her think that, and how did she know what was happening?

It was strange that Jennie Lee found herself comforting her grandmother, as her gram carried her around the kitchen and cried. "Everything's going to be okay, Grammy. I will take care of everything." These are the words that came out of the little girl's mouth. Did she understand what had just happened? Had the girls been prepared for this event?

In the next moment, Jennie Lee disappeared! How could she take care of everything then disappear? Had she forgotten something important?

Jennie Lee didn't really disappear, but she did feel as if half of herself was gone. She would never see her sister again—her twin who was always there, her twin who ate with her, played with her, slept with her. How could Jennie Lee live without her other half?

The townsfolk came together to grieve with the family for the little girl who had just died, but where was Jennie Lee? Was she there? Did she hear? Did anyone try to comfort her? Did anyone think to talk with her about the accident? Perhaps they did, and Jennie Lee just couldn't remember. Perhaps the events were so traumatic that the little girl decided not to remember what just happened…Jennie Lee just simply forgot. She turned her thoughts inward to her heart to find the answers. Jennie Lee did not remember her twin's funeral. She could not remember if she ever saw her sister again. She had no memory of her birthday two weeks later or summertime. Was there Thanksgiving and Christmas that year? She hardly remembered starting school the following fall. What Jennie Lee did remember was waking up!

One day, after she had turned nine years old, she found herself sitting on her favorite rock in the front yard. She blinked her eyes and pinched herself. "Ouch! That hurt!" she yelled. What had just happened? Jennie

Lee never felt like this before. It was as if she had returned home from a very long journey! Jennie Lee knew that she hadn't really left home but felt like she had been away, visiting someplace.

"Oh, I'm so very happy to be alive! I love my home and family! Thank you for letting me live on Earth!" Jennie Lee was very excited, but what were these new feelings?

The little girl was a changed person. She felt old and wise, like her grandmother. She felt protected by two special angels, one on either side of her, holding her up. Jennie Lee knew that life was good, and she wanted to live to be one hundred years old! In her heart, she knew that Georgia Ruth was okay, that no one ever really dies. They just…go "Home."

How did Jennie Lee know this? Who told her these things? Why did she feel such peace around her? She thought and thought. She thought about things she had never asked before: why are we born, and why do we die? Do we really die, or do we go someplace? Why are we here? Why can't I remember what has happened these last four years? Did I go away? She didn't know the answers to these questions until she grew up. And while she was growing up, she read many wonderful books. Jennie Lee met warm, loving people who helped her find the answers. This is the story of what might have happened after Georgia Ruth died…

As Jennie Lee comforted her grandmother, her twin sister appeared before her in a corner of the kitchen. On either side of her stood two very tall angels; a very pretty lady with long wavy hair, and a chubby man with only a little hair. They were all surrounded by a bright white light!

"Come with me," Georgia Ruth said, holding out her hand to her sister.

Jennie Lee looked at the outstretched hand. Georgia Ruth was standing in front of her, but she knew that was not true. Georgia Ruth was being taken to the hospital at that very moment. She frowned. "I don't understand."

"Come with me," Georgia Ruth repeated, looking into the mirror of her twin's face and reaching with her outstretched arm.

Jennie Lee's eyes grew big with wonder. She stretched out her right arm and touched the tips of Georgia Ruth's fingers. How warm she felt! Instantly, Jennie Lee was standing next to Georgia Ruth! Jennie Lee turned around, and there she was, in her grandmother's arms. What in the world was happening?

"Don't worry," Humphrey the angel, said, smiling at the girls. "It will be okay. You'll see."

"We must go," urged Muriel, the other angel. She took the girls by the hands.

In a second, they were gone. In the next moment, they were standing in a very busy place! Everything was very bright and beautiful! The colors of the sky, the streets, and the people's clothes were more vivid than either child had seen before. Trees and flowers were growing along the sidewalks, which were pearly white. Jennie Lee thought she might be in a city because this place was so big! But the roads shimmered with cleanliness. There was activity all around them.

People were everywhere! There were cars, buses, grown-ups, and children going this way and that. Jennie Lee was frightened that they would be hurt standing in the middle of a huge street. The angels stood on either side of the twins, then suddenly, all four of them were hovering in midair. They didn't even fall! They were observing all of the action from above the scene!

"How did you do that?" Jennie Lee asked.

Muriel and Humphrey gave each other a knowing look and laughed. "It's magic!" they chimed.

"Then, where are we?" she whispered.

"Why, we're in Heaven," Humphrey replied, sweeping his hand across the whole scene. "Heaven is the name that you know, but it is known by many other names, too."

"Did you think it would be quiet?" Muriel asked.

"I never knew it was really here," Jennie Lee said.

"Sure you did," said Georgia Ruth, who had been very quiet up until now. "You just don't remember."

"This is Georgia Ruth's new home," Muriel said quietly.

The twins looked at each other. They both swallowed hard.

Georgia Ruth squeezed her sister's hand tightly. "I'm sorry I have to go," she whispered to her sister. A teardrop splashed down her cheek.

"But why?" Jennie Lee cried.

Muriel bent down and put an arm around each little girl, hugging them tightly. "Don't you remember our meetings?"

"No!" Jennie Lee sniffed, wiping her eyes on her sleeve.

"We met before while you were sleeping," Humphrey explained. "We have talked many times about this day."

"Yes," said Georgia Ruth. She looked at her twin. "It's true. We talked about it just three days ago. I was going away, and you were staying with Mummy and Daddy." She rubbed her hand up and down Jennie Lee's back to comfort her.

"But I don't want you to go!" Jennie Lee yelled defiantly. No one was going to take away her twin!

"Georgia Ruth stayed with you awhile, and now she has a very important job to do here," Muriel explained gently. "This was decided before you came to Earth. She is going to help other children cross over. Let me show you…" Muriel swept her arm around as the whole scene changed.

"What does it mean to *cross over*," Jennie Lee asked, still clinging to her sister.

Her eyes grew as big as saucers watching the busy street fade away. In its place appeared a beautiful yellow building. Beside it was a magnificent playground full of happy children. The girls had never seen such a wonderful sight. "Ooohhh!" they both squealed. The grass was a brilliant green. It grew underneath all the equipment on the playground no matter how much the children ran and tumbled on it. The twins didn't recognize all of the playthings, but some were familiar. There were children swinging and sliding down slides! They were climbing on the monkey bars or playing tag! Some were blowing giant bubbles while others were playing hopscotch. Everyone was laughing or singing—no one was sad!

Humphrey said, "Some of these children have left earth to live here in heaven, and others are getting ready to leave heaven to go and live on Earth. That is called 'crossing over.'"

"But I don't remember this!" Jennie Lee shouted.

"Yes, you do. Think!" Humphrey declared, staring into her eyes.

Jennie Lee was swept back in a swirl of clouds. "Remember!" She heard in the distance.

They were playing in the sand on the beach, two small children. One held a shovel while the other plopped a pail of sand at the water's edge. The iridescent sand sparkled.

"It's time to go back to Earth," one said to the other.

"I can't. I have work to do here," the bolder one said as she bent over to shape the pile.

"We must! We have to!" argued the first, gathering a pail of water.

"You can do it better without me. Besides, I couldn't stay long if I did come. You know this. Those earth years are so short!" the second little one stated. "I have work to do here."

"But it would be so much fun!"

"If I came, I could only stay five earth years. What good would that do?" The little girls stood up.

"It would teach Mummy and Daddy that life goes on and on. We could be twin sisters and learn our lessons together. Please, please?" The little one wrapped her arms around the other.

"Oh, all right!" Laughing, the child again bent over, picking up her shovel. She filled another pail with sand and turned it upside down. "But that's a very hard lesson for some people to learn."

"Uh-huh, but everyone needs to know this. Many people don't know that we live on and on. We just pass from one world to another."

The second child stood up and stretched. She looked at the other. "And what of you, my sister? If we go down there as twins, I'll have to leave you there. You'll be torn apart, and my heart will be heavy."

"Yes, I know, but maybe it will push me to do more studying about why we go to Earth. You know I've been lazy these past years. I promise that I'll be strong; there are those I must help. I have my lessons to learn. We must all learn to love each other. We must learn to live together in peace if we are to care for our planet."

"You're right, of course. We've been together forever, but I'm already grieving for the time when I will have to leave you."

The two children kissed each other, hugging tightly. The days in front of them would be difficult and most painful for the one left on earth. In heaven's time zone, earth years were merely days; but to someone living on earth, it could be an eternity.

The little girls walked hand in hand away from the seashore. They looked up as seagulls drifted by on the breeze. Pure joy existed in the air, and the girls couldn't be unhappy even if they wanted to. This was going to be just another adventure!

"Will you look in on me once in a while?" The first little one asked.

"You know I will, but I'm not sure you will know this. Remember that we have to forget about Heaven when we go to Earth, or we'd never learn the lessons that we've chosen. The shock of my passing will affect you more than you think. It will take you years before you'll realize this. My leaving will also affect the way you relate to our family and friends. You'll constantly be looking for that which you lost. You'll never feel our special bonding again."

The children faced each other. The one who would be Jennie Lee sighed, "I have a lot to learn about earth love. I really wanted to learn the lessons with you. Does it have to be this way?"

"No, it doesn't," the one who would be Georgia Ruth answered. "You could stay here and help me instead of going back to Earth," she said.

"And if I do that, what will I learn? The lessons here are different ones," Jennie Lee stated.

"Yes, everything we do is a learning experience. We never stop learning, no matter how old we are," Georgia Ruth sighed.

Looking at each other was like gazing into a mirror for the role of twins was one they had played before. And even though both twins felt differently about their future, their optimistic outlook on life echoed each other.

"We all need to learn the lessons of life," Jennie Lee's arms opened wide. "There are so many things to learn and so much to enjoy about the earthly existence! Do you know that there are people there who don't even know that all things—plants, animals, earth, and rocks—need to be respected and cared for? They don't realize that we are all one! We are part of each other! Plants and animals are becoming extinct because people don't care that they are destroying them! All living things benefit each other. They have a right to life. Someone has to spread the word!"

"And that would be you, my sister?" Georgia Ruth smiled as she sat again on the sand, watching the ocean waves crash along the shore. "Earthlings don't yet understand how important our world is, or how it relates to the universe. We're very happy here, but how many on Earth really know what Heaven is like? We forget this life when we go there. We all have to be at our best so that we can help each other as much as possible. We must learn that all people around the world are the same. Our job is to work together to make the world a better place to live in, then they would see how beautiful life really is."

The children hugged each other as the scene faded, and Jennie Lee awakened. She blinked her eyes as the confusion started to leave her. She remembered the day she and her twin built the sandcastle on the beach. It seemed like it had been a hundred years ago.

Muriel bent down and placed a hand on Jennie Lee's shoulder. "You see, my daughter, there is no death; life goes on continually. When a person dies on earth, he or she just leaves their earth body and comes back *home* to live and regroup. This is where we review our life's work. Many people on the planet believe that their soul goes to heaven when they die, but it is hard to understand because the person they love is no longer there. We need to teach everyone that there is no death, just a change. Maybe you can help. Do you think you would like to see what Georgia Ruth will be doing?" she asked quietly.

For a minute, she thought it was all a dream. Jennie Lee wanted to wake up in her own cozy bed with her twin right next to her. Maybe if she saw where her sister would be, she wouldn't feel so sad. At least Georgia Ruth was still holding her hand. "Yes," she sniffed.

The loving angels gently directed the girls to the front entrance of the big yellow building. The stairs shimmered in white marble. The huge double doors opened easily into a large hallway. The walls and floors gleamed with freshly polished wood. It smelled like a forest as they entered inside. Tall doors lined both sides of the hallway. They could hear voices echoing from other rooms.

The girls were ushered through the first door on the right. It was a large office with a beautiful L-shaped mahogany counter dividing the room. This was a room full of activity! There were file cabinets everywhere and stacks of brightly colored folders on each desk. The twins felt like they had entered a very big school!

"Each colored folder is a different age group of children," Mrs. Bridges explained.

The girls looked up to see a kind-faced stout lady standing at the counter.

She picked up a green folder. "This is Georgia Ruth's folder," she said. "Was it traumatic, darling, crossing over?" she asked Georgia Ruth.

"No!" Georgia Ruth exclaimed. "One minute I was there, and the next I was here!" She shrugged her shoulders in wonder.

Muriel and Humphrey looked at each other, smiling.

"But, oh my! Jennie Lee isn't due here for a long time!" Mrs. Bridges looked from one twin to the other.

"Jennie Lee wanted to see what her sister would be doing," Humphrey said, patting Jennie Lee's shoulder.

"You two are so indulgent!" Mrs. Bridges exclaimed with a twinkle in her eye.

"It's hard for Jennie Lee to understand right now. We're trying to ease the pain as much as we can," Muriel added.

"I understand," Mrs. Bridges sighed as she came around the corner. "Life on earth can be tough, but it goes on. Come, girls, I want to show you something." She held out her hands as each girl took one.

On the other side of the room was a lovely alcove. A long window seat sat underneath a ten-foot high arched window. The diamond panes sparkled as the bright sun poured through the glass.

"Sit with me for a minute, dears," she urged as she seated herself.

The soft cushion was covered in a diamond pattern of greens and wines, reflecting the pattern of the windows. The girls crawled up on the cushion beside Mrs. Bridges, and gazed out of the window. The lawn was a brilliant green, seeming to go on forever. Magnificent wildflowers in every color of the rainbow dusted the edges of the lawn.

Georgia Ruth pointed at a bunny that was darting between the bushes. She giggled at her sister.

Jennie Lee smiled for the first time since the accident. "Is that bunny dead or alive?" she asked.

"Why, alive, of course! You see, love, when all creatures come here to Heaven, they get well again, just like people. Remember that animals have their purpose on earth, too. There is no real death. Once you finish your job on Earth, you come here and go on with your life. It is merely the end of one life for another."

Jennie Lee shrugged her shoulders and held out her hands. "I don't understand."

The stout lady drew her onto her lap, giving her a big hug. "You see, my dear, dying is just a beginning, not an ending. There must be a way for you to travel from Earth to your real home when you finish your job, so they call it dying."

"Then why can't we just visit back and forth the way I'm doing now? Or can't I go back either?" As the thought passed through Jennie Lee's mind, she started to worry. Was she really going back to Earth?

Mrs. Bridges looked at the child; her eyes grew misty as she realized what this little girl was going through. She wanted to make sure that what she said would be clear to Jennie Lee. They were taking away her sister, and the twins would not see each other again for a very long time. How could she make this simple?

"If you could remember your life here after you go to Earth, you wouldn't want to stay. You see, there is always joy and laughter here, never sadness. We are always surrounded with love. But we go to Earth to see what it's like if we don't live with happiness all the time. We appreciate love more if we experience what it's like to live without it. Now, let me go on. Hmm…you have two bodies: your earth body, which is human, and your spirit body. Your earth body is made up of your skin, your bones, organs, muscles, blood vessels, and lots of other parts that help you live in that world. You can run, play, go swimming, eat, and sleep with the help of your human body. Your spirit body is the part of you that is constantly learning. It is the real you. Now, when you crossover, you leave your human body on Earth because you don't need it here. Georgia Ruth has done that, but her spirit body is always with her. You can do whatever you want here without a human body. You can still run, play, jump, or skip without it. While you are visiting us, you are in your spirit body too. Your earth body is well because you'll be leaving here soon and going back to earth. This visit is like a dream. You may still visit here in your dreams. Earth is your learning place, your school, and that is where you belong."

"But why?" the girls asked in unison.

"Because when you decided to go to Earth, you both signed up to learn different things. It was all decided before you left here. Jennie Lee, you wanted to learn many lessons, also teach some. Georgia Ruth, you decided to learn just a few things at this time. Do you remember?"

"Not really," she said.

"That's all right. You'll remember soon. Girls, look out of the window again."

Both girls stood on their knees, gazing out of the window. In place of the lawn stood their home and the surrounding marsh.

"Oh, look!" Georgia Ruth said. "It's Pine Island! Look! There's the river and our uncle's house. I see children playing."

It was her brother, Bruce, climbing up an apple tree covered with blooms. Could she really smell the apple blossoms? A little girl was sitting on a rock in front of the house.

"Who is that?" Jennie asked.

"Why, that's you, of course!" Mrs. Bridges laughed. "Remember, you're still living on Earth. This is just a visit to help you understand. And that's your earthly body. Look over there, dears." Mrs. Bridges pointed to the front yard. Sitting on the lawn was a blue baby carriage. "You have a new baby sister—Kimberley!"

Both girls looked surprised, then Georgia Ruth smiled.

"Oh, I remember her. We met shortly before we left here! I'm beginning to remember."

"Yes," Mrs. Bridge nodded her head. "I'm glad you're beginning to remember. The whole family met here before you went to Earth. Families are decided ahead of time to set up certain lessons to be learned, then it's up to you. Everything takes time on earth. Now, Georgia Ruth, let's see what you'll be doing here."

The three left the alcove and stepped out into the hallway. Humphrey and Muriel were talking with a group of children whose ages ranged from four to fourteen years old. Each held his or her own colored folder.

Suddenly, Georgia Ruth's eyes lit up brightly! Squealing delightedly, she hurled herself at a young boy who was standing with the group. He was tall and slim, with soft brown eyes that seemed to reflect the wisdom of the ages. He laughed and threw his arms open wide.

"Georgia, it's about time! I wondered when you were arriving!" He swept her up in his arms, hugging her tightly. "What did you learn on earth? You were only there a short time. Are you ready to get to work, partner?" he laughed as he swung her around.

"I learned to ride a pony, and that life is good! Now I remember what I'm supposed to do. I missed you, Seth!" Georgia returned his hug enthusiastically. She had forgotten about her old buddy. She and Seth had worked together before with the children of heaven. "How is little Katie Winslow?" Katie was a little girl who had gone to earth to learn what it was like to be disabled.

"Katie is an inspiration, but she doesn't know it yet. She's in a wheelchair, and her parents have just got her a specially trained dog to help her out. She's been very sad, but her new dog will bring her much happiness. She's beginning to do well in her studies. Someday, Katie will help many disabled people learn that they can live good lives. We'll peek on her soon. Next case, please!" Seth remarked, giving her a squeeze.

Jennie Lee felt her sister pulling away. Georgia Ruth's soul, her spirit, was beginning to break the bond that held them together. She was beginning to realize that her sister truly had another job to do. Very soon, she knew that they would be parting.

Mrs. Bridges looked down to find Jennie Lee gazing at her sister and Seth.

"In Heaven we are all adults and eventually understand all that is going on. You're beginning to see that your twin's job here will be as important as your job on earth, aren't you?"

Jennie Lee nodded slowly. She could feel herself letting go inside. She sighed deeply.

Seth put Georgia Ruth down, then the two of them walked over to Jennie Lee.

"The important thing about 'crossing over,'" he explained, "is that we try to help people understand why they are going to Earth. Then we try to help them adjust to life here in Heaven when they return. Some people's experiences or lessons are to be learned in a short amount of time. Others have decided to learn many things. They will stay on earth a very long time. It is up to you to make that decision before you go. We try to learn in a certain amount of time, just like your schools on earth—once you learn all the lessons in first grade, then you graduate to second grade. But in an earth lifetime, that could be a day, month, year, or many years. It's very hard to learn all about love or other teachings in one lifetime."

Georgia Ruth took her twin's hand. "I do remember now!" she said breathlessly. "I want to do this job! I'll learn so much from Seth and the others. This was all planned before I went with you to be a twin. We'll be able to help so many people learn about the sweetness of life. Some travelers will have it easy, but others will have a hard life because of their circumstances there. Many won't see that life is worth living for the little rewards—the sunrise and sunset, warm days, cool evenings. They won't see the stars telling stories at night. They won't travel to our favorite beach to smell the salt air or make sandcastles. You must help me, Jennifer."

It was the first time Georgia Ruth had ever called her by her full name.

"You chose to stay, and I chose to go. It won't be easy for either of us. We must face this; we'll have to part soon. Think of our earth home like summer camp; you'll be away for a little while. You help me on Earth, and I'll help you here in Heaven. We'll be partners, too, you and I, even if you don't remember."

Georgia Ruth wrapped her arms around her identical twin, a mirror reflecting a vision of two little girls enclosed in the protective light of God. "We'll see each other again shortly. It'll seem like only a few short weeks even after one hundred years! And we'll be twins again; you must believe this. Without even knowing it, you'll help many. You'll be able to comfort others when they need it. Your kindness to animals will be greatly appreciated in their world, even if we can't hear their words. You'll be a great comfort to me also, knowing that you're on earth doing a good job. I will be right here helping you when I can, giving you advice. And I'll be learning and listening to you too." She stepped away from Jennie Lee. "It's time to go…"

Jennie Lee looked around her, at all her wonderful new friends who had helped her to understand. She hadn't expected that five earth years would have passed so quickly. "Life is so very precious," she whispered. And you've all been so kind. I don't want to leave, but I guess I have to. Will I do a job just like this when I come back?"

Mrs. Bridges answered her, "Why, of course you will! But don't forget there are many wonderful jobs to choose from. By the way, what are you going to do when you grow up on Earth? Look at all the fields you could study. Why, you could be a teacher or writer, a doctor or judge, a famous actress or pilot! How will you choose?

Jennie Lee smiled and shrugged her shoulders. "I think maybe I'd like to teach that life never ends, and that death is only a change, like the leaves falling," she said quietly.

Muriel bent down and laid her hands on both girls' shoulders. "It's time to say goodbye."

The girls faced each other for the last time in this lifetime. The mirror had started to crack as their souls began to separate. A soothing calmness settled over the twins as they hugged and kissed each other.

"I won't say goodbye for we'll see each other shortly, even though you'll be very old. Don't you know this?" Georgia Ruth lifted her hand, brushing Jennie Lee's hair out of her eyes. "You can visit in your dreams sometime. Maybe Humphrey and Muriel will take us on adventures!"

The two angels looked at each other, rolling their eyes, but nodded to both girls.

Jennie Lee felt her own strange yearning, telling her it was time to return to her home on Earth. "I know in my heart that this is right, but it's still hard to understand. I have to leave, and you won't be there; you have to stay here. It'll be hard going on alone." She started to cry.

"But you must help everyone," Georgia Ruth held her sister's hand. "Especially Mummy and Daddy. They need to learn that life goes on and no one ever really dies. Kiss them for me. Tell them I love them and will miss them. Grammy and Uncle too! We're only separated for a little while, then we'll be together again. Think of the fun we'll have telling each other what we've learned."

"I'll try to do my best; you know I will. I love you, Georgia. I'll miss you." Jennie Lee ran her fingers along the sides of Georgia Ruth's face as if she were afraid that she would forget what her sister looked like.

"If you forget," Georgia Ruth laughed as she smiled at her sister, "just look in the mirror; I'll be there."

"I'll be there, I'll be there, I'll be there…" faded in the distance. Jennifer awoke to find herself sitting on her favorite rock in the front yard. What a strange feeling! She felt so alive! Had she been sleeping all her life?

Jennifer breathed deeply. She could almost taste the salt air of her home on the marsh. Was this the first time she had ever done this? She looked up at the fluffy clouds in the sky, wondering what she was doing on Earth. She was very happy to be alive and living here! She pinched herself; was she really alive? "Ouch! That hurt!" she yelped. Blackie, her dog, trotted over to see what was happening. Jennifer buried her face in the dog's fur, hugging her tightly. She wanted to remember Blackie's scent, and the touch of her course fur. Was she touching and smelling for the first time?

Jennifer felt something else—the presence of two angels, one on either side of her, holding her up. She couldn't remember Humphrey and Muriel, but she knew the angels were there beside her, and all was well with the world.

Somehow, she knew she had grown up. Jennie Lee was no longer there. In her place stood Jennifer, straight and tall. There, by her side, stood Humphrey and Muriel; invisible to her but still comforting her. They would stay with her until they felt she was ready to be on her own. Jennifer knew instinctively that they were there. She didn't need to see them, she just believed. She could not remember the visit that had taken place with all her new friends, but she knew that something mysterious and wonderful had happened.

Jennifer tucked Georgia Ruth in a special corner of her heart where she could visit when she felt lonely. She missed her sister tremendously but knew that Georgia Ruth was okay, and life goes on. She would see her sister again someday. Right now, life was an adventure to be lived! There were so many things to do; where would she start? Maybe she would take piano lessons soon…

Life is full of different lessons to learn while we are here on Earth. We shall work together to make it a better place to live. Some of us will live many long years here while others will have a shorter time to do their jobs. Remember, too, that just because a life is short doesn't mean that the mission wasn't completed. Perhaps Georgia Ruth's mission was to teach that life, like a circle, is never-ending.

Jennifer grew strong as she accepted her sister's passing, but she was sensitive always. All living things grew precious to her. She made lots of friends and kept them through to her adulthood because it was so important to her to keep them. Georgia Ruth was right when she said Jennie Lee would look for that special bonding of twins but never find it. That was the hardest lesson to learn.

It is a tragedy when someone loses a loved one through death, but the stronger a person becomes, whether child or adult, the smaller the wound grows. Your twin brother or sister will always be with you. Your special loved one will also be with you always. Honor them by talking about them. It helps to take away the pain and keep their memory alive within you.

Our spirits go on forever. In the spirit world of Heaven, everyone is busy, just like here on Earth. Life is an education. As Seth said, think of life as a school: once you learn all the lessons in one grade, you graduate and go on to the next.

Our twins and loved ones will be waiting for us on the other side. We want to make them just as proud of us as we are proud of them. Let us be good and kind to one another all over the world as we grow up and go on with our lives. They would want it that way.

It's just the beginning…

ABOUT THE AUTHOR

Jennifer Hills Lutz

Jennifer is a former English teacher and holds a degree in Interior Design. She also specializes in color healing, herbs, and essential oils for health. Her interests include writing, music, quilting, and exploring spirituality. In 2021 she will become a Lay Minister for All Paths to God, a Religious Science New Thought organization.

Jennifer has spent a lifetime studying the truth of our existence since she lost her identical twin at 5 years old. This delicate tale is her personal story; "when my twin passed, I went into a fog that lasted for four years. When I emerged from that fog, I knew right away that Georgia was not dead—she was just 'over there.' I also knew that all was well with the world, and that those two special angels were on both sides of me, holding me up. I started asking questions: 'what happens when we die? Where do we go? Do we live on?' No one could answer my questions, but my dear grandmother started handing me books—wonderful books about the philosophy of life after death. I have spent all my life pursuing this subject. My readings have comforted me while I formed my own opinions of what I think is truth.

"May this tale of grief and enlightenment spur you on to learning your own truths, taken from your life experiences, and may your journey of discovery and wonder bring you great joy."

Jennifer has also produced an audio CD of her book and gives lectures on Life After Death. She divides her time between West Florida and South East New Hampshire.

Connect with Jennifer via email: authorjhlutz@gmail.com